W9-BVI-251

APR. 0 5 1996

14.95

DUE DATE

CLOSE-UP
A Focus on Nature

SILVER BURDETT PRESS

© 1995 Silver Burdett Press
Published by Silver Burdett Press.
A Simon & Schuster Company
299 Jefferson Road, Parsippany, NJ 07054
Printed in the United States of America
10 9 8 7 6 5 4 3 2 1

Library of Congress
Cataloging-in-Publication Data
Hunt, Joni Phelps, 1956-
    A chorus of frogs/by Joni Phelps Hunt; pho-
tographs by A. Cosmos Blank . . . [et al.].
        p. cm.--(Close up)
    ISBN 0-382-24870-8 (LSB)
    ISBN 0-382-24871-6 (SC)
    1. Frogs--Juvenile literature. [1. Frogs.]
I. Blank, A. Cosmos, ill. II. Title. III. Series: Close
up (Parsippany, N.J.)
QL668.E2H96 1994
597.8'9--dc20   94-30871
                                                       CIP
                                                        AC

A CHORUS OF FROGS

WRITER
Joni Phelps Hunt

SERIES EDITOR
Vicki León

PHOTOGRAPHERS
A. Cosmos Blank, John Cancalosi, Stephen Dalton,
Michael Fogden, Jeff Foott, Martha Hill, Stephen J. Krasemann,
Alex Kerstitch, Kevin Schafer, Kennan Ward, T.A. Wiewandt,
Doug Wechsler, Art Wolfe, Belinda Wright, Norbert Wu

DESIGNER
Ashala Nicols Lawler

SILVER BURDETT PRESS

© 1995 Silver Burdett Press
Published by Silver Burdett Press.
A Simon & Schuster Company
299 Jefferson Road,
Parsippany, NJ 07054
Printed in the United States of America
10 9 8 7 6 5 4 3 2 1

THOSE RIBBETING FROGS...

They hop. They leap. They swim. They burrow. They climb trees. They catch crickets in a single bound. And they croak. Oh, how they croak!

Because they are humble, often hidden little creatures, we usually think of frogs as wet, green pond residents. But they can be wildly colorful. A few can live in the desert. Their fascinations include parenting behavior and prey-catching abilities. And their change from eggs to tadpoles to frogs is one of the most visible and wondrous transformations in the animal kingdom.

Frogs have been around more than 200 million years. During that time, they've forged an important link in the food chain and close ties with the environment. The status of frogs worldwide tells us much about the condition of our planet's ecosystem.

DOUBLE BUBBLE

A short-headed frog in India, at right, croaks at twice the volume as he forces air into double vocal sacs. A frog calls alone to declare his territory or in a group chorus to attract a mate.

The eyes have it! Frogs' eyes vary in shape, size, and color. Many have an unexpected beauty, as does the eye of a desert spadefoot toad, below.

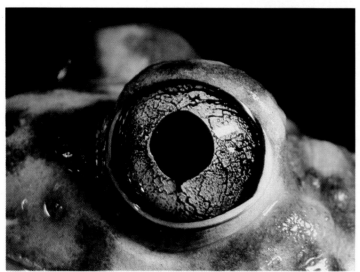

WHAT IS AN AMPHIBIAN?

A Greek word meaning double life, amphibians live both in water and on land. Frogs – called Anura or tailless ones – are most numerous with 3,600 species, including toads. The remaining 500 or so amphibians belong to the Caudata order of salamanders and newts and to the Apoda order of wormlike creatures called caecilians.

An amphibian is a coldblooded or ectothermal vertebrate: its body temperature changes with its surroundings, and it has a backbone. Its thin skin lacks fur, feathers, or scales. Instead of shells, amphibian eggs have a jellylike coating and require water or moisture while developing. After hatching, the young usually grow up in water, using gills to breathe. As adults, most amphibians have lungs and can lead a double life on land and in water.

rogs live almost everywhere on earth. They're sensitive to temperature and humidity and must have fresh or slightly salty water.

In temperate climates located between the tropics and the polar caps, frogs live in or near ponds, swamps, and streams, or in forests and fields. In winter their body systems slow down to protect them from the cold. Frogs in the world's deserts stay in burrows most of the year to escape heat and dryness.

The largest number of species live in the tropics, where the climate stays moist and warm. Some are colored brightly to warn predators of their poisons. A few spend their entire lives in rainforest trees.

A typical frog has a short, squat body. As with most animals, a frog's shape, size, and body parts differ to suit its home and lifestyle. All toads are frogs, but often they look different. Toads have heavier bodies and cannot jump as well as other frogs. They have rough, sometimes warty skin. Bumps behind their eyes called parotid glands and other skin glands secrete poison to discourage predators.

TELLTALE HEART

Glass frogs of tropical America are known for their see-through skin. But the bare-hearted glass frog, above, is more transparent than most. Males often babysit their young, keeping them damp and protecting them from predators.

BOTH SIDES NOW: From top to bottom, frogs are poised for action. Toe discs like those silhouetted on the treefrog to the left help frogs get a grip on life. Strong hind leg muscles stay ready to rocket a frog into air or water at the first sign of danger or a tasty tidbit. Both the arrow-poison frog, top, and red-eyed treefrog, above, live in Central and South America.

PETAL PUSHERS

Whether on a rose, above, or on fungus, right, these U.S. treefrogs have pigment cells that change their skin color. Darkness, low temperatures, and high humidity cause their natural color to darken, absorbing heat and light. Sunny days lighten the skin to reflect heat. A Pacific treefrog can change color in about ten minutes, a barking treefrog in 30 minutes or more.

Found in rainforests, the smallest frog measures only one-half inch in head and body length. The largest – at one foot – is the goliath frog of Africa. Most frogs average two to five inches, not counting their legs.

Front legs support a sitting frog and are used by males to clasp a mate at breeding time. The longer, muscular back legs can launch frogs into leaps on land and propel them in water. Treefrogs have toe discs that stick like suction cups for climbing and maneuvering in tight places.

Frogs use their limbs for balance and movement but usually not for snatching food. That's done by the animal's sticky tongue. It's connected at the front and lays back toward the throat. When an insect comes within range, the frog flips its tongue out to catch it. The frog grabs larger meals with its mouth.

Once captured, prey is swallowed alive and whole. A frog's teeth are too small to use for chewing, but they keep the meal from crawling back out. To help push prey down its gullet, the frog lowers its eyes into the roof of its mouth.

The male's mouth is designed for calling. With tightly closed nostrils and mouth, the ribbeter pumps air between its mouth and lungs. The air makes a vibration or croak as it crosses the vocal chords. Some air goes through two slits in the floor of the mouth into a vocal sac. Air resonates in this pouch and turns up the croak volume. The voice of a single male proclaims his territory. Groups of males compete in a loud chorus to attract mates. Females have no vocal sacs and are usually silent.

Frogs are thin-skinned creatures, with good reason. Their lungs need help supplying enough oxygen, so their skin takes it in through blood vessels close to the surface. Frogs don't drink water. Their skin absorbs it as they sit in a pond or puddle, or even in damp soil in the case of toads. With air and water passing through, the skin dries out easily. To help keep it moist, special glands produce a mucus "moisturizer" that makes frogs feel slippery.

Bulging, beautiful frog eyes come in colors from berry red to orange to greenish-yellow to dark with gold flecks. The pupils can be round. Or they can be a vertical or

horizontal oval, or even diamond shaped. A frog can't see much that's in front of its nose. Small moving objects less than a foot away are out of focus but are perceived as food anyway. Eyesight is clearer at three or four feet, and frogs can spy large predators at ten feet. As well as eyelids, they have transparent membranes to act like goggles underwater.

Frogs can also hear when submerged. Most have a circular eardrum, called tympanum, set behind and below the eye. Keen hearing is especially important at mating time when frogs follow calls of their species to the breeding pond.

Tadpoles and aquatic frogs have small pits in rows along the body called a lateral-line system, left over from their ancestors. Cells in the pits pickup vibrations in the water to help the animals sense wave motion or the approach of predators.

BREATHING EASY: **What comes in also goes out of a frog's skin. Frogs take oxygen from air and water into the skin and release carbon dioxide. This exchange of gases works best on a soft, wet surface like this granular glass frog's skin or the inside of a human's lung.**

PONDERING THE NEXT MOVE

A hop, splash, and a jump. Frogs do that and more. Moving in water, on land, and through air are a frog's basic means of defense. In human terms, track and field athletes do well to jump their own heights. In frog terms, a typical bullfrog jumps 20 times its body length. Some tiny species may leap 40 times their length. The one-foot-long African goliath frog jumps proportionately less – only about nine feet.

A few species of treefrogs quickly cover a distance about 100 times their body length by gliding from tree to tree. A web of skin between the toes acts like a parachute to slow their descent. The Asiatic gliding frog holds its long webbed toes stiff to glide 40 or 50 feet. On takeoff from a high tree branch, it soars diagonally down, with some control over the length and direction of the glide. A relative, the flying frog, sails from tree to tree in the rainforests of Borneo.

When hunting food, earthbound frogs can move in less spectacular ways. Some toads crawl after food. British natterjack toads run in quick bursts on short back legs in their sandy seaside homes. Some frogs even creep or stalk almost on tiptoe.

HIDE-AND-SEEK

Venezuelan arrow-poison frogs, far left and below, may look as inviting as the plants they're on, but their deadly skin poisons keep predators away. The Peruvian horned frog, left, uses a threat display to discourage attackers.

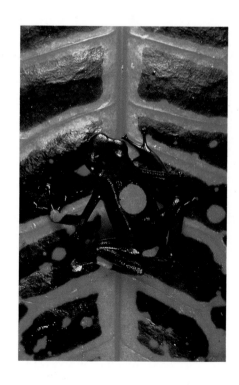

nsatiable – that best describes a frog's appetite. The rule of thumb seems to be that if it moves – and it's smaller – grab it! Frogs aren't discriminating eaters except when they find poisonous hairy caterpillars or beetles with large pinchers. They consume living worms, crustaceans, spiders, and insects. Larger species with strong jaws, like the South American and Malaysian horned frogs, also dine on birds, small reptiles, mice, and even other frogs.

Cane toads were originally sent to Australia and other islands as a pest-control device. They hunt at night, but the sugar cane beetles they were brought to eat are active during the day. So the toads dine on nocturnal frogs and other small animals. When local mammals and reptiles try to eat a non-native cane toad, they're poisoned by its skin toxins.

Frogs have many enemies and little body strength to defend themselves when confronted. Their strength lies in avoiding predators: snakes, hawks and wading birds, mink, otters, bats, rats, hedgehogs, foxes, domestic cats, raccoons, skunks, turtles, large fish, and others. A frog's best defense is its powerful hind legs.

When fleeing or hiding don't work, some frogs play dead. Herpetologists, scientists who study reptiles and amphibians, believe the animals are literally scared stiff – into unconsciousness. If the deception works and the predator leaves, the frog soon recovers and hops away.

The European toad uses another ploy when threatened by a snake. The toad puffs air into its body and stands on tiptoe so it looks too large for the snake to swallow. Sometimes it works, and the snake leaves.

THAT'S A MOUTHFUL!

Much of a frog's life is spent catching prey and avoiding predators. In a frog-eat-frog world, a horned frog gobbles a spadefoot toad, top left. At lower left, a frog pursues a meal with its tongue out for the catch. A rear-fanged snake works at gulping down a rain frog, above.

Protective coloring lets many frogs disappear into their surroundings. Glossy green leaves, shrubs, bark, dead leaves, dirt, rocks, colorful tropical plants, lily pads, or bulrushes – concealers all.

Neon colors worn by tropical frogs warn predators away. The skin glands of some of the smallest frogs of Central and South America produce a bitter-tasting poison strong enough to paralyze a small animal. Known as arrow-poison or dart-poison frogs, they hop about without fear during daylight. The ants they feed on help them produce the strong toxins.

The Asian fire-bellied toad and European yellow-bellied toad have bright green, brown, or grayish coloring on their backs. When threatened, they turn up their legs and head to show bright red, orange, or yellow warning colors on their undersides.

If no other means of defense works, some species give a shrill scream much like a human scream. This startles a predator and gives the frog time to escape.

LET'S GO TO THE HOP

TURF TUSSLE

Two male strawberry arrow-poison frogs, only about one-inch long, wrestle over territory in Costa Rica. Fights may last more than an hour, with brief interruptions as one frog breaks away to call. The other attacks him, and the contest continues. By claiming a territory as its own, an arrow-poison frog ensures a food supply and a safe place to breed.

A native tribe continues to hunt these highly toxic frogs, roasting them, and using their poison mucus to coat blowgun darts. Poison from one frog tips 15 arrows or darts. Each dart can paralyze a bird or small monkey, which the tribe hunts for food.

Frogs play the mating game with countless variations. In temperate climates it's usually in spring. In dry climates it's during seasonal rainfall. In the tropics frogs mate several times a year. While most eggs are laid in water, some are laid on land, some in trees. Those that breed in water often return each year to the same site. Some researchers believe the scent given off by algae may be the draw. Warm weather makes algae grow faster. Since tadpoles feed on algae, this may tell adult frogs when it's breeding time and which pond to choose.

Males usually reach the pond first, migrating after dark in small groups. Toads hop to it both day and night, increasing the risk from predators. In Britain, toads move in large groups and travel up to one mile, being choosy about the pond. During migration, they go around walls and other obstacles. Since many are killed while crossing roads, volunteers dig toad tunnels under roads or collect and carry some safely to the other side.

The closest male frogs come to courtship activities is a big bachelor party. Large groups of suitors get together and bellow in a chorus, beginning in early evening and on into the night. Croaks are loudest on overcast days with high humidity. Each species has a different call, with a specific pitch and tone. Usually a single note, the call is short and repeated quickly. Besides the familiar "ribbet" or "jug-o-rum" calls, frogs can sound like a bee buzz, bird trill, cat purr, dog bark, chicken squawk, chick peep, duck quack, lamb bleat, and more. Other frogs have been likened to a hammer pounding an anvil, a snore, a banjo, or a foghorn. When heard in chorus, the sounds may be in harmony or just a loud din.

Once a female locates her species' choral group, a male hops on her back, clasping her behind the front legs or around the waist. This tight grip is called amplexus. So he won't slip off, the male's front toes develop rough swellings, called nuptial pads.

A female may reject the breeding site her mate chooses. She hops off in search of another, with her suitor getting a free ride. A study of gray treefrogs in the southeastern United States showed females often chose another pond.

They went where their eggs and the growing tadpoles
would face fewer predators and have more to eat.

Seemingly, the female has little choice as to which
male becomes her mate. She is attracted to the deeper
voices of large males. Several may clasp her at once and
end up fighting. The larger, stronger suitor usually wins.
Some toads simplify the process. The female makes her
choice and then nudges him to get his attention.

Most breeding activity takes place in the dark, so cases
of mistaken identity do occur. If a male grabs another
male, the latter croaks a warning and wriggles free of the
amorous embrace. If a male of one species clasps a female
of another, he can usually tell by her size and the way
she moves that he's got the wrong mate, mate.

A pair stuck together in amplexus rarely come unstuck, even when threatened. In water the male may try to speed their escape by paddling his feet from his perch, but it does no good. It's up to the female to save them.

Once she's found the right site, the female frog may begin laying eggs or wait several hours or days. Depending on the species, a frog may lay as few as one or two large eggs or as many as 30,000 small ones in a season. Frogs breeding in ponds lay many more eggs than species laying on land because potential dangers to the young are greater.

In ponds or other bodies of water, a female lays eggs and the male adds sperm over them to fertilize and allow them to develop. Water causes the jellylike substance around the egg to swell two or three times its original size. The jelly helps the eggs stay moist and offers some protection from predators.

The way eggs are laid depends on the amount of oxygen available. Warm ponds without much oxygen are favored

CALL OF THE WILD: Males of each species give a specific call, which can sound like a frog, a barnyard animal, or a man-made noise. Their choruses attract not only females but predators too. Tungara frogs of Central America often avoid moonlit nights, choosing the safety of cloudy, wet ones instead. They also prefer to join large choral groups – a safety-in-numbers approach. Masked puddle frogs usually call while hidden in vegetation beside a pond.

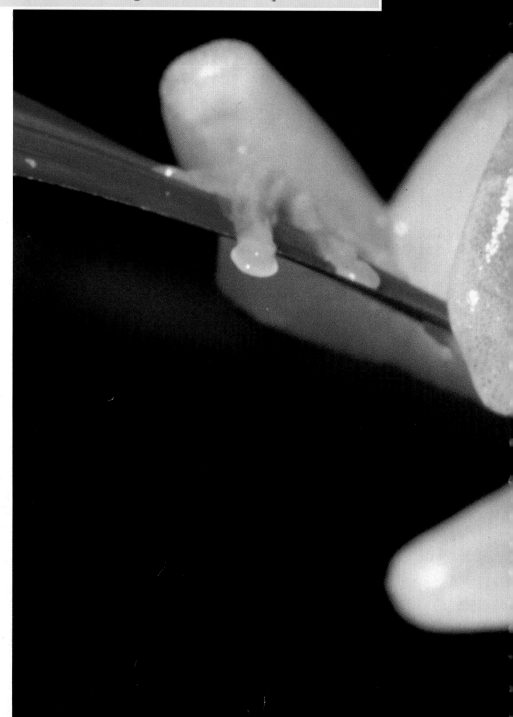

AMPHIBIOUS ASSAULT: Clad in olive and red hues, female golden toads seek out the soft purring trills of the male chorus line – only to be besieged with suitors. Living in the Monteverde Cloud Forest Reserve in Costa Rica, the toads used to appear when heavy spring rains filled their breeding pools. In recent years none have been sighted.

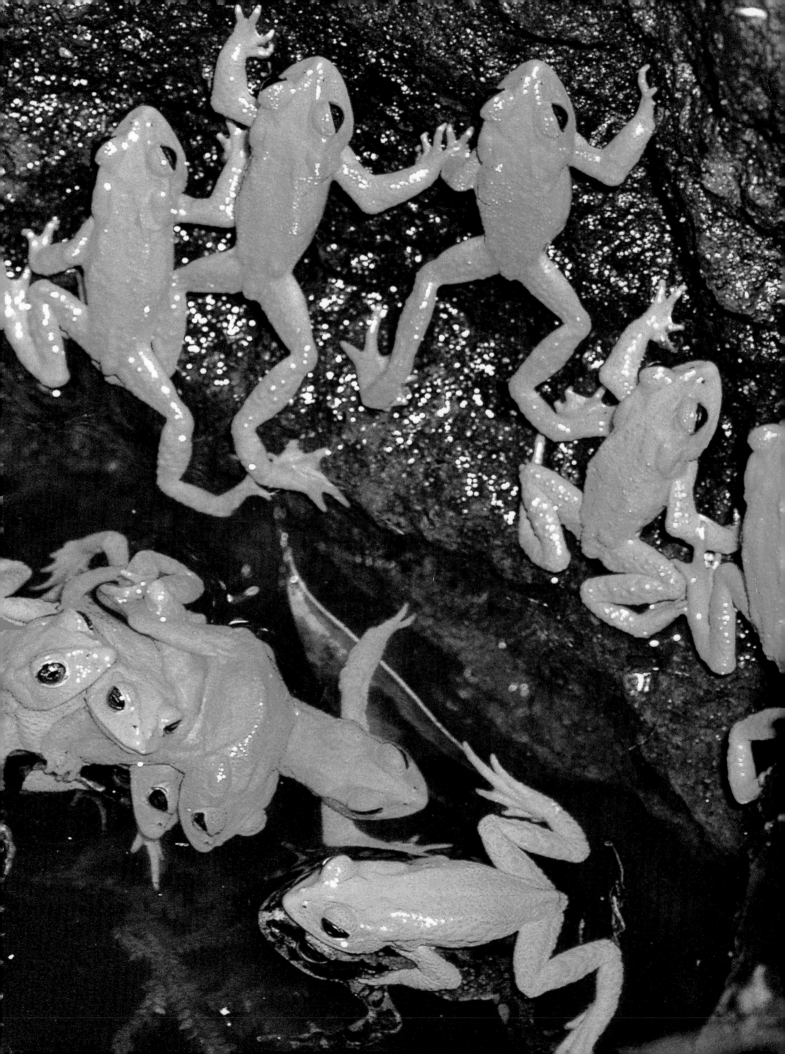

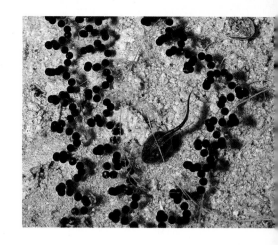

by toads. They lay in long spread-out strings. Frogs lay in flat masses on the surface of warm ponds. Strings and masses let lots of water and oxygen reach the eggs. In colder ponds with plenty of oxygen, frogs lay large clumps massed together and attached to plants underwater. After laying eggs, the female leaves the pond and goes on with life. The male of many species stays at the breeding area to find another mate.

Many frogs lay their eggs on land. Several species of treefrogs in the American tropics lay fewer than 40 eggs on leaves of bushes or small trees overhanging streams. High humidity and rainfall help keep the eggs from drying out while the tadpoles develop inside. After about two weeks they've grown strong enough to break through the egg membrane, fall into the water below, and survive.

Leaf frogs of Latin America use several laying strategies. During rainstorms, males call from tree branches. Once a male clasps a mate, she carries him down the tree to a pond formed by rain. They sit in the

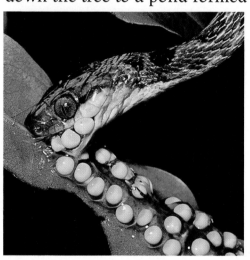

water for ten minutes while the female takes in water, then climb back into the branches. The female lays her eggs on a leaf over the water, and the male fertilizes them. She covers the eggs with water, causing the jellylike coating to swell and keep them moist. The pair repeat the process, including a trip to the pond, three to five times. If the newly laid eggs aren't moistened, they dry out and die.

Another species of leaf frog uses its hind feet to fold a leaf around just-laid eggs, forming a small nest. A more elaborate nest with several leaves is built by leaf frogs using unfertilized eggs as glue to hold the side together, to plug the ends, and to give moisture to the developing tadpoles.

Frogs throughout the world also build nests of mud or foam. In China the male fairy musician frog selects a site less than a foot above a small pond, where he digs a mud

FROM THE BEGINNING

Clutched in amplexus, the golden toad pair, far left, release and fertilize a double strand of eggs, suspended like a string of tiny pearls. Above, spadefoot toad eggs must develop quickly before their shallow pool evaporates or hungry tadpole kin devour them. A cat-eyed snake does just that to red-eyed leaf frog eggs, at left.

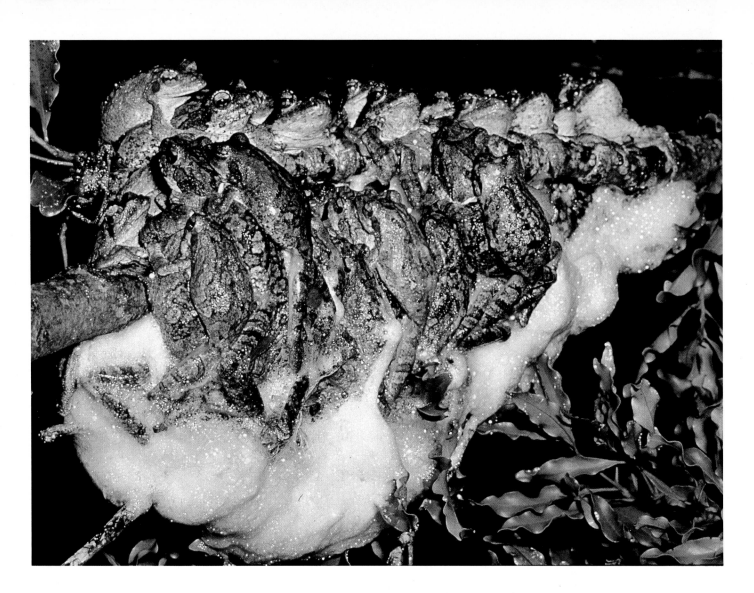

nest with his snout. He then utters a lilting flutelike call to attract a mate. The female lays about 100 eggs in watery jelly, which supplies moisture as the tadpoles develop. Rain soon washes the young into the pond to finish growing.

The male smith frog of tropical America makes a large mud nest at the edge of a pond by hopping in a big circle. He pushes mud up around the depression for walls, patting them into place with his front feet. If he needs more mud, he goes underwater and brings some up on his snout. Once the nest is nearly finished, the smith frog begins his trademark call, a sound like a hammer striking an anvil. After a brief courtship, eggs are laid in the nest. There they can develop, walled away from predators in the pond. Nests are built close together, so males often fight over territory. They dunk foes, wrestle with their legs, and stab each other with bony spines on their front feet.

ALL IN A LATHER

After a long drought, nearly 40 African foam-nesting frogs gather on a tree branch above a pond to breed, above left. Females secrete mucus, and the group kicks it with their hind legs, whipping air into the foam. Like beating egg whites into meringue, the froth becomes stiff. Jelly-covered eggs laid on the foam are covered by more foam. The outside of

Some frogs in Australia, South America, and Africa build foam nests. They can be found in trees, in water, on shore, or in a burrow. In burrow nests, fewer eggs are laid because chances of the young surviving are greater. Heavy rains flood the nest and release the tadpoles.

The African burrowing frog uses a burrow without the foam. Unlike most burrowing frogs that dig with their long hind legs, the African or pig-nosed frog digs with its shovel-shaped snout, kicking dirt away with its short hind legs. The female begins the burrow near a pond, stops to find a mate, and continues digging with the male clasped to her back. After the eggs are laid and fertilized the male digs out of the burrow. The female stays to sit with the eggs. Less than two weeks later tadpoles hatch, the mother digs a tunnel to water, and the young wriggle to the pond.

Frogs make full use of their environment. For instance, a tree fork with water in it can hold a tadpole. Damp moss near mountain streams works well for some Australian species. In the forests of Borneo, eggs laid in shallow puddles in logs turn into frogs in about 17 days. One African species flattens and squeezes itself to lay eggs in broken bamboo or between the leaves of wild banana plants. When the eggs hatch, well-developed tadpoles have jaws to eat small insects, other frogs' eggs, and plants. Tropical American and tree-dwelling frogs deposit eggs in bromeliads, plants whose centers hold water like cups. The eggs are laid with a substance that thickens the water and reduces evaporation.

the nest hardens, while the inside stays moist. Tadpoles hatch in three to four days, wiggle to make a hole, and drop into the pond about two days later, above right.

The South American male tungara frog kicks up a foam nest in shallow water. By the time tadpoles are ready to leave the nest, water around it has often evaporated. So tadpoles won't be left high and dry, they use their muscular tail to flip back into water.

While most frogs lay and fertilize eggs and then abandon them, about ten percent stay to help their young survive. The male glass frog of the American tropics babysits eggs clustered next to him on a leaf. He protects them from predators and keeps them moist with water from his bladder.

The South American surinam frog uses an unusual parenting approach. Living on muddy river bottoms, the surinam has a flat, crablike appearance and beady eyes. Its long front toes feel along the river bottom and shove food into its mouth. The back toes are webbed.

TO BOLDLY GO: Suspended in a watery world, tadpoles spend all of their time looking for food. They search for tiny organisms such as algae and protozoa by rooting around water plants or in mud. Many tadpoles will eat dead or injured animals in the pond, including relatives.

HIDDEN ASSETS

The female pygmy marsupial frog of Venezuela, below, carries six or seven large eggs in a pouch on her back. When tadpoles are ready to emerge, she opens it at a small pool or water-filled bromeliad.

The male surinam attracts a mate underwater by clicking noises rather than croaks. While the pair swim around with the male holding on, the female's back skin swells. Finally they swim near the surface, turn and somersault back to the river bottom. During the descent the female releases eggs, which the male fertilizes and pushes into her swollen skin. The somersaults continue for two to three hours until 50 to 100 eggs are stuck onto the mother's back. Her skin swells to encase the eggs in about ten days. As the eggs develop, the mother goes on with life. About ten weeks later, fully formed little frogs pop out of her back.

Several species of treefrogs use similar methods to incubate their eggs. The female leaflike marsupial frog carries her young in a pouch on her back until fully formed froglets emerge – without ever being in water.

Hatching young is not the sole responsibility of the mother in frogdom. In the forests of southern Chile and Argentina, the female Darwin's frog lays 20 to 30 eggs in damp moss or leaf litter and goes away. Several males guard the eggs until the tadpoles begin to move. Each male then scoops up eggs with his tongue and swallows them. They fall through the slits into his vocal sac, where they remain until completely grown. When papa opens his mouth, out hop tiny frogs.

The male midwife toad of western Europe plays nursemaid to a string of 20 to 60 eggs that he entwines around his legs. To protect the eggs, he hides during the day. At night he looks for food and dampens the eggs with dew or shallow water. When the eggs are ready to hatch about a month later, the male dips his legs in water and the tadpoles swim off.

Females in at least five species give birth directly to froglets. Eggs go through tadpole and metamorphosis stages inside the mother's body. This is the ultimate insurance against predators.

QUICK-CHANGE ARTISTS

Perhaps more than any other animals, frogs grow and change before our eyes. Transparent eggs allow us to watch as tadpoles form. After they hatch, we see tadpoles grow and change shape until they're ready for the final big switch to frogs – a process known as metamorphosis.

The time it takes for a frog to grow varies by species and environment. A frog egg laid in water changes to a tadpole in as little as 36 to 58 hours. The top part of the egg is alive and growing. The yolk at the bottom supplies food. At about eight hours old, a digestive track forms; at 13 hours the nervous system takes shape. Gills start to show, a tail bud grows, and a mouth forms. Around 28 hours old, the embryo hatches from the egg jelly and hangs by its mouth onto the jelly or plants.

ALL ABOARD!

Arrow-poison tadpoles squirm onto mom or dad's sticky back, above. Some are carried to ponds and released. A few species leave young in water-filled bromeliads, where mom returns every few days with food. Another carries its tadpoles until they become frogs, puddle-soaking them when needed.

PEEK-A-BOO

Few frogs develop like a rain frog does. The female lays several large transparent eggs, like those above, on damp leaves or moss in the Costa Rican cloud forest. Each egg holds enough nutritional yolk for the young to develop into a tadpole and then into a froglet. A horny spike on the froglet's nose frees it from the egg capsule.

After five hours the hatchling begins to move. At 1½-days old the heart beats, blood runs through gills, and eyes develop. When blood circulates in the tail a day later, the brown or black animal looks like a tadpole. At four days, skin covers the gills, and it can swim, eating algae and plants.

As if growing up isn't hard enough, tadpoles face many dangers. Most frogs lay hundreds or thousands of eggs just so some will survive hungry predators. They include water insects such as water beetles, dragonfly nymphs, and water scorpions. Other predators are fish, ducks, wading birds, spiders, and snakes. Some tadpoles, such as those of the meadow tree frog and spadefoot toad, also eat frog eggs and other tadpoles.

Aside from the dangers of being eaten, tadpoles compete with thousands of others for food. If a pond is too crowded, some species release a growth inhibitor to stall competitors' development. Diseases and water mold can kill eggs or tadpoles. Heat or drought can dry up a pond. Heavy rains flood ponds with mud, and silt can bury the food supply. For every tadpole that becomes a frog, hundreds die.

How does a fishlike tadpole with a tail and no legs living in water become a frog with four legs and no tail living on land? Although it seems about as likely as a princess kissing a frog and taking home a prince, it happens all the time.

The change in form – or metamorphosis – from tadpole to frog happens quickly. Land species change faster than those that live in water all the time; desert dwellers are quicker yet. What tell-tale signs indicate metamorphosis has begun? Small hind legs appear, and then front legs. The tail grows shorter, absorbed by the body as food. Lungs develop and gills disappear. The froglet's larger mouth now has a tongue and small teeth. The animal is carnivorous, eating insects, invertebrates, and other small amphibians. Eyes become large and bulging, all but a trace of tail disappears, lungs breathe air, skin toughens, adult coloring appears, and legs strengthen.

After metamorphosis, a frog grows rapidly for about two years. Then it grows slowly. How old do frogs in the wild live to be? It's hard to tell because frogs are difficult to track, and most frogs don't die of old age. In captivity, larger frogs live longer, ten or more years.

THE BIG CHILL

ince a frog is a coldblooded or ectothermal creature, its internal temperature rises and falls with the thermometer. If body temperature goes too far below its normal range, a frog can't function. In temperate climates when the weather turns cold, the animals become sluggish and unable to quickly leap away from harm. To survive predators and to keep from freezing, they hibernate either at the bottom of a pond or in a moist burrow. Heartbeat, respiration, and other life functions slow almost to a stop.

PRESTO-CHANGE-O
Leopard frog tadpoles in Arizona, above, go through metamorphosis at different rates. The one with front legs will be a froglet sooner. Risk of attack from predators increases when legs appear and the tail is still in place. At that point, they can neither jump nor swim well.

31

Frogs must also escape intense heat. Spadefoot toads found in Europe, Africa, Asia, and North America use the hard spade-shaped growths on their hind feet to burrow to moist ground. In the hot, dry deserts of the American southwest, Couch's spadefoot lives underground about 75 percent of the year. While in the burrow, its body functions practically shut down, a process called estivation. The toad needs only 20 percent of the oxygen it would if active. Its thin skin absorbs water and oxygen from the soil. Sometimes layers of shed skin form a cocoon around the toad to keep its body moisture from evaporating. During rainy periods in July and August, the desert dweller emerges and gorges on insects, storing energy for its coming sleep.

Since they lead a sheltered life, Couch's spadefoot toads have whirlwind courtships. The sound of thunder lures the toads out of their burrows with the promise of a summer rainstorm heavy enough to form large pools. Soon a large chorus of males attracts females, and eggs are laid that night. Eggs hatch in two days, and tadpoles begin eating anything – plants, tiny aquatic animals, or other tadpoles. Food is scarce, and they must grow quickly before the pond evaporates. When the pool is almost dry, spadefoot tadpoles cluster together and wiggle their tails to dredge more water out of the mud. A little more water can save their lives. Metamorphosis speeds up to just a few hours from when front legs appear to when the toadlet leaves the water. Usually the cycle from egg to spadefoot toad takes about three weeks, less if temperatures are high.

Like the spadefoot, the water-reservoir frog of Australia lives many months underground and comes out during heavy rains to breed. As its name suggests, the frog stores rainwater in its body while in estivation. Aborigines often dig the frog out of its burrow for needed water.

WELL BALANCED

Whether the size of a dime or a dinner plate, frogs possess remarkable coordination. Sticky toes and quick reflexes let them perch on the flimsiest twig, lily pad, leaf or flower.

LEAPIN' LEOPARDS! A North American leopard frog shows off fine leaping form in its pond environment. A frog olympics of sorts, held every year in California, commemorates Mark Twain's story, "The Celebrated Jumping Frog of Calaveras County."

HANG ON!

Scientists have begun efforts to protect frogs worldwide. The habitat of the Madagascan tomato frog, near right, is endangered. White's treefrog, far right, is holding its own in its native New Guinea and Australia.

People throughout the world eat frog legs, with an average of 15 animals used per serving. The French alone consume about 400 million legs annually. European countries now protect local amphibians, so the market for frogs has shifted to Asian species. India and Bangladesh export more than 150 million frogs for food each year. With fewer frogs to eat mosquitoes and crop pests, India must use pesticides to lessen the risk of malaria and maintain crop yields.

FROG PRINCES

Humans and frogs go back a long way together. Ancient cultures and tribes used frog toxins for hunting and for recreational hallucinogens, strange as it sounds. Scientists today use frogs for research on cancer, ulcers, muscle regeneration, and the immune system.

Frogs may be trying to tell us something about our planet. An indicator species, frogs are more directly exposed to substances in the environment – water, air, plants, animals – than most creatures. Scientists believe a link exists between the increase in pollution and the decline in frog populations around the world.

Since the 1970s, the disappearance of frogs has accelerated. Golden toads in Costa Rica and gastric brooding frogs in Australia's rainforests have apparently vanished. Once-common U.S. species like the spotted frog in Oregon and leopard frog in Nevada, and the Japanese rice-paddy frog are nearly gone. A survey in one region of Brazil found six species extinct and another seven of thirty species in decline.

Natural fluctuations in population cannot account for losses in so many species. Frogs are even disappearing in parks established to protect them. Their decline is due to a combination of factors. First, habitat is disappearing. Ponds and wetlands are drained, silted, or bulldozed for construction. Forests are cut for timber. Open land is used for agriculture, and water levels drop as fields are irrigated. Drought also reduces habitat.

Pollution takes a heavy toll. Ponds contain fertilizers, pesticides, and heavy metals. Acid rain and snow taint water sources. The thinning ozone layer is thought to affect frogs at high altitudes in the Andes, Alps, Rockies, and Sierra Nevada. Herpetologists worldwide are searching for ways to better protect them. A computerized "frog log" database gathers information about all amphibians and helps to uncover reasons for population declines.

As individuals, we can help frogs by preserving their environment. Keep a small garden pond for them. Watch them grow and change where they live instead of taking them where you live. Appreciate them in the wild rather than on a dinner plate. We all have a stake in what happens to these fragile creatures in their rubbery wet suits.

ABOUT THE PHOTOGRAPHERS

A. Cosmos Blank/Photo Researchers: page 14 lower
photo
John Cancalosi/DRK: page 14 upper photo
John Cancalosi: page 31
Stephen Dalton/Photo Researchers: pages 2-3, 34-35
Michael Fogden/DRK: pages 5, 7 lower inset, 10-11,
13, 15, 17, 18-19, 20-21, 22, 23 lower photo, 24, 25,
26-27, 28, 29, 30, inside back cover
Jeff Foott: page 23 upper photo
Stephen J. Krasemann/DRK: page 7 upper inset, 33
Alex Kerstitch: pages 38-39
Kevin Schafer and Martha Hill: title page, 6-7, 37
upper left, back cover

Kennan Ward: page 8
T.A. Wiewandt/DRK: page 4 lower photo
Doug Wechsler: page 37
Art Wolfe: inside front cover, page 9, 12, 13 lower
photo, 32, 37 upper right, 40
Belinda Wright/DRK: page 4 upper photo
Norbert Wu: front cover

ABOUT THE AUTHOR

Joni Phelps Hunt brings her experience as a
writer and editor, plus a fondness for frogs and
puns, to *A Chorus of Frogs*. She would like to thank
the chorus that inspired her. Joni was the author
of Blake Publishing's book, *The Desert*.

SPECIAL THANKS

Dr. David C. Cannatella, University of Texas at
  Austin
Linda Countryman, Docent, Los Angeles Zoo
Harvey Fischer, Curator of Reptiles, Los Angeles Zoo
Sue Schafer, Assistant Reptile Curator,
  San Diego Zoo
Paige Torres

WHERE TO SEE FROGS

The best place to see these amphibians is in their
natural environment. Frogs live in cities as well as
rural areas – just listen for them on overcast or rainy
days or nights. Most zoos have frog exhibits, usually
in the reptile house.

TO LEARN MORE

BOOKS

Frog and Toad Watching, by David Webster
  (Messner, 1986)
Frogs and Toads of the World, by Chris Mattison
  (Facts on File, 1987)
Frogs, Toads, Lizards, and Salamanders, by Nancy
  Parker and Joan Wright (Greenwillow, 1990)

FILM

It's A Frog's Life (Oxford Scientific Films, 1989)

Your steady gaze has watched
dinosaurs and civilizations come and go.
Now pollution threatens your home, your life.
What kind of world would it be
without your voice to herald spring?